Additional Praise for *Stumbling Blocks*

"The wonderful eloquence of these poems testifies to the traf[...] new. The speaker is a witness, a visitor, a participant in the life o[...] [...] city or Rome. But there is far more. Above all, these are poems of a continuous, crafted subtlety, voicing in each poem the way the fragile present moment not only reveals the past but rescues it. This is a book that will give endless pleasure and illumination to the traveler in every poet, and the poet in every traveler." —Eavan Boland, author of *Woman Without a Country*

"Reading Karl Kirchwey's new book, one comes across the line in a poem entitled "Argos": *Every morning in the park of broken statues / a group of dog walkers gathers*. It is a casual observation, but holds modestly within itself many of the elements of these marvelous poems. Here, in this poem and many others, topography is fluid; time blurs under the force majeure of the poet's erudition, and the lucky adventurer is ensorcelled by the passing characters and circumstances that readily succumb to Kirchwey's attentions. Throughout this short collection, the author maintains a languid, generous presence. He is a master of his craft and a reliable guide through the shadows of Rome and beyond. In *Stumbling Blocks*, Kirchwey is writing at the peak of his powers, which are considerable." —Daniel Lawless, founder and editor of *PLUME: A Journal of Contemporary Poetry*

Praise for Karl Kirchwey's Previous Works

On *Mount Lebanon: Poems*

"Expertly crafted throughout, this book attests a consummately cultured, thoroughly contemporary poet." —Ray Olson, *Booklist*

"With its tight structure and deft language woven onto a loom of history and mythology, the poetry maintains the kind of gravity and allusive depth T. S. Eliot dreamed of. It is as if Kirchwey spilled a bit of Frazier, Faulkner, Joyce, and H.D. and let it run joyously through the veins of his imagination." —Taylor Hagood, *The Rumpus*

On *The Happiness of This World: Poetry and Prose*

"Kirchwey is at his most accessible, political, and strong, writing poems that beg to be heard." —*American Poet: The Journal of the Academy of American Poets*

"[These] poems bring together music and feeling with a skill that few of his contemporaries can match." —Ilya Kaminsky, *Library Journal*

"Kirchwey has been a poet more respected than cherished; with this vivid collection, that may change." —*Publishers Weekly*

On *At the Palace of Jove*

"The poems shimmer with intelligence, wit, and delicacy; and yet at times they resonate with the deepest and most stirring of feelings. Kirchwey manages with exemplary grace to bring vividly to life the world of the classical past as fully as his twenty-first century experiences." —Anthony Hecht

"Kirchwey achieves a cool formal grandeur, rich in slant rhymes and sly humor. His verse shimmers, shaking dust from classical themes." —*TimeOut New York*

"These confident, witty, and often surprising ruminations brave both the large, unwieldy junctures (between art and life, stability and chaos, memory and forgetting) and more singular concerns (youth, beauty, loss, remorse)." —*New York Times Book Review*

On *The Engrafted Word*

"Kirchwey skillfully mingles images of the ancient world with those of the modern, uncovering in antiquity an intimate present." —*The New Yorker*

"Elegant . . . [poems] that engage both the head and the heart." —Mary Jo Salter, *New York Times Book Review*

"Kirchwey has become even more profoundly the elegiac poet of places and sited moments . . . One of the very best poets of his generation." —John Hollander

On *Those I Guard*

"Finely contemplative . . . distinctive and distinguished." —Richard Wilbur

On *A Wandering Island*

"Painterly craft and a feeling for the omnipresence of drama are everywhere in this accomplished first book. Its rendering of the textures of pleasure and dismay, the way things fall apart or flow together—whether in the half-obliterated past or the passing instant—discloses a poet of sumptuous resources." —Amy Clampitt

STUMBLING BLOCKS

Also by Karl Kirchwey

STUMBLING BLOCKS

BLOCKS

ROMAN POEMS

Karl Kirchwey

TRIQUARTERLY BOOKS/NORTHWESTERN UNIVERSITY PRESS

EVANSTON, ILLINOIS

TriQuarterly Books
Northwestern University Press
www.nupress.northwestern.edu

Printed in the United States of America

10 9 8 7 6 5 4 3 2 1

Library of Congress Cataloging-in-Publication Data
Names: Kirchwey, Karl, 1956– author.
Title: Stumbling blocks : Roman poems / Karl Kirchwey.
Description: Evanston, Illinois : TriQuarterly Books/Northwestern University Press, 2017. |
    Poems, some previously published. | Includes bibliographical references.
Identifiers: LCCN 2017017770 | ISBN 9780810136274 (pbk. : alk. paper) |
    ISBN 9780810136281 (e-book)
Subjects: LCSH: Rome—Poetry.
Classification: LCC PS3561.I684 S78 2017 | DDC 811.54—dc23
LC record available at https://lccn.loc.gov/2017017770

To the memory of Pina Pasquantonio

Unto you therefore which believe *he* is precious: but unto them which be disobedient, the stone which the builders disallowed, the same is made the head of the corner,

And a stone of stumbling, and a rock of offence, *even to them* which stumble at the word, being disobedient: whereunto also they were appointed.

—I PETER 2:7–8

Let us not therefore judge one another any more: but judge this rather, that no man put a stumblingblock or an occasion to fall in *his* brother's way.

—ROMANS 14:13

CONTENTS

Acknowledgments　　xi

A Fatal Hand　　*3*

I

Thought Experiment　　*7*

Leaving　　*8*

Airbus　　*9*

PATER ∘ FILIO ∘ FECIT　　*11*

Body and Mask　　*13*

On the Janiculum, January 7, 2012　　*15*

II

Roma 8F 9260　　*19*

Janiculum Passage　　*21*

Tiber Island　　*22*

Janiculum Staircase　　*24*

III

North Frieze Block XLVIII, Figures 118–20　　*29*

The Stones at the Circus Maximus　　*30*

A Pair of Fountains

　1. Ask a Question　　*32*

　2. Starry Crown　　*33*

Stumbling Blocks: For Pius XII　　*35*

IV

Troia	*39*
Stromboli	*40*
Aeaea	*42*
Argos	*44*
Circe	*45*

V

A Letter from Istanbul	*49*

VI

Santa Cecilia	*59*
Chiaraviglio	*61*
A Roman Garden	*63*

VII

Santa Maria in Trastevere	*67*
Two Farewells	
1. A *Narcissus*	*68*
2. Villa Aurora	*70*

VIII

Gentle Joyous God	*75*
Reading Apuleius	*76*
Pentecost	*78*

IX

Fiumicino, Morning	*81*
Ostia Antica	*82*
A Return	*84*
Roma città aperta	*86*
Notes	*87*

ACKNOWLEDGMENTS

The poems in this book have appeared or are forthcoming, sometimes in different forms, in the following journals and websites, to the editors of which grateful acknowledgment is made.

Arion: A Journal of Humanities and the Classics: "Pentecost," "Stromboli"

The Atlantic: "A Roman Garden"

Columbia Magazine: "Argos"

E-Verse Radio: "A Fatal Hand" (as "Du Bellay Sonnet 27")

The Hudson Review: "A Narcissus"

Literary Imagination: "Stumbling Blocks: For Pius XII," "Tiber Island"

Little Star: "A Letter from Istanbul"

The New Criterion: "Ask a Question" (as "Roman Wall Fountain"), "Starry Crown" (as "Roman Fountain")

New England Review: "Janiculum Staircase," "Santa Cecilia"

The New Republic: "Body and Mask," "Ostia Antica"

The New York Review of Books: "Aeaea," "Fiumicino, Morning"

The New Yorker: "Troia"

Parnassus: Poetry in Review: "Circe," "Santa Maria in Trastevere," "Thought Experiment," "Villa Aurora" (as "Sestina: A Valediction")

Plume Poetry 5 (print): "The Stones at the Circus Maximus"

Plume Poetry 3 (print): "A Return" (as "Redemption")

Poetry Northwest: "Leaving" (print), "On the Janiculum, January 7, 2012" (online)

Slate: "Reading Apuleius"

Southwest Review: "Roma 8F 9260"

The Yale Review: "Airbus," "Chiaraviglio," "PATER ∘ FILIO ∘ FECIT," "*Roma città aperta*"

"Gentle Joyous God" appeared in *Irresistible Sonnets*, edited by Mary Meriam (Headmistress Press, 2014). "Starry Crown" (as "Roman Fountain") was featured on *Poetry Daily* (October 13, 2016).

Many of the poems in this book were written during the three years I served as Andrew Heiskell Arts Director at the American Academy in Rome. To all those with whom I made that journey, I offer thanks for their conversation and their friendship.

My thanks to Parneshia Jones for her interest in these poems. And to Tamzen Flanders, for her intelligence, patience, and love, I owe my deepest debt of gratitude.

STUMBLING BLOCKS

A Fatal Hand

Rome astonishes you, who contemplate
the ancient pride that once outfaced the skies,
audacious hills and shattered palaces,
the walls and arches, baths and temples—yet
consider how time's power to devastate
block on grand block has had another purpose,
supplying living masons at their labors
with antique fragments to incorporate.
Then look again, and understand the way
Rome sifts the strata of her own heyday,
rebuilds herself from many divine works:
you will conclude the demon of the land
endeavors once more with a fatal hand
to resurrect these broken dusty bricks.

    —from the French of Joachim du Bellay, *Les Antiquitez de Rome*,
Sonnet 27 (1558)

1

Thought Experiment

Caesar's last breath, a half-liter of air
exhaled that day in the Roman Forum,
still circulates around the earth somewhere,
after the blood and daggers, so every time
I breathe, it is five molecules, or ten,
of Caesar's breath in its entropic state
inspire me, allowing for those fallen
into the sea or used to light the cigarette
of a man in Boston who was homeless
in weather hovering around twenty degrees
to whom at dusk I gave the dollar bill
I had found on the sidewalk in L.A.
when the rising sun had made an appliqué
of palm crowns across Gehry's symphony hall.

Leaving

All day long the wind spoke
in a language I could not understand,
an aimless heave and surge of feeling
high in the branches of the trees.
The leaves in swags braided and unbraided
as at an altar where something was gathered
then scattered, indifferent to the cost.
My son sat nearby on the patio,
sketching my daughter as she read,
and his hand partook of that pitched silence,
the headlong rush and stall of it,
restless partings and rifts of shadow
closing suddenly and without appeal,
a choice offered, then withdrawn forever—
until I heard my own journey announced.

Airbus

In a dove-gray nave
    (the leather seats are blue),
      being hour after hour resigned to
the perfect boredom of

their own passage, in a hush
    that is hardly devotional,
      but in which the soul,
captive only to its wish

to be elsewhere, feels the roaring
    and brutal friction of it,
      five hundred knots
across each naked fairing,

they have drawn the shades deep,
    as if to spare themselves from
      the sight of Elysium,
its brilliances of cloudscape,

where hooded Bruno walks,
    taught by fire, and Borromini,
      drawn forever upward by
his own ideas' helix:

all those who have built,
    according to their certainties,
      somehow in that high place,
appareled in daylight

—even the boy once led
    down the narrow aisle
    to the realm of gauge and toggle
over which presided

those who signed his book of life
    and gave him a silver pin,
    worthless now, but for one
whole day, he counted himself

a king of infinite space
    and, returned through the cockpit door
    to his mother and father,
in each blind and loving face

read his eventual landfall,
    at what vague bay or winter-brown
    forest at afternoon
he can no longer tell.

PATER ∘ FILIO ∘ FECIT

In the deep tranquility of the courtyard,
    dizzy with jasmine's smell,
    the plush sibilance of gravel,
and the sound of water in a braid

from the young Hercules strangling a serpent,
    I look again to the carved marble bench
    where two tin-hat doughboys crouch
(killed in France), and I see the sand bucket

on your head at the age of two.
    Your childhood now ended, and wars distant,
    your life ready, that was meant,
it seems, for the world—yet may I keep you

always from the center of my gaze,
    and therefore most fully cherished,
    most dearly apprehended,
like vision in a darkened place,

or the inconspicuous inscription
    on a lapidary wall, where
    WHAT A SON SHOULD DO FOR A FATHER
THE FATHER DID FOR THE SON.

Remembered time and its agony—
    WHO LIVED ELEVEN YEARS
    FORTY-EIGHT DAYS AND TEN HOURS—
I carry it always with me,

as if to reckon your days with a claim
　　　made invulnerable by its knowledge of
　　　the precise term of mortal love,
undeceived by this place and its calm.

Body and Mask

In the Villa Doria Pamphilj,
    I saw a carved plaque set into a wall,
    quite unremarkable,
just the usual *lotto di putti*,

the contest between cherubs, but then I
    saw that one of the two
    had wriggled his way somehow
inside the mask of tragedy,

the way a dog might flail blindly,
    its forequarters stuck in a paper sack,
    but more cunning than that, and not stuck,
having crawled in deliberately

(in the same way an apprentice of Cellini
    hid his lover inside a bronze head of Mars,
    her nude flank like the whites of its eyes),
the cherub's buttocks protruding impudently,

and one arm reaching, as if in play,
    through the mask's gaping mouth-hole
    toward ripe fruit in a bowl,
intentional and greedy.

On the far side of quince, plum, and cherry,
    I noticed the other,
    his face ajar with horror.
What he had thought dead was alive, clearly,

that plump arm like a tongue, obscenely
    determined to remain among
    the pleasures of the living:
so that to say the tragic contains comedy,

or to marvel over the way
    what is dead, done, finished off
    may yet startle by its galvanic life,
its instinctive reaching for joy,

still misses the point of this ordinary
    lesson cut in Luni marble,
    which concerns instead the inevitable
fit of body and mask, their strange intimacy.

On the Janiculum, January 7, 2012

Earth has not anything to show more fair,
and you'd have to be dead inside not to feel something—
but what, exactly? There are scholars who could tell me
about the walls, arches, baths, and temples, and
it's not that I'm indifferent to such knowledge,
but long ago I learned to follow beauty.
The city lies flushed by sunset in its bowl,
the snow mountains on the far horizon like a dream,
as runnels of violet invade each street,
and what is left, on a winter afternoon,
is a feeling of joy so closely followed by grief
you might almost miss the moment of tenderness
in which both resolve, as if toward something vulnerable:
though the city does not have you, has never had you, in mind.

11

Roma 8F 9260

There was an antic parade not long ago:
    dozens of Fiat 500s, the windup toy car,
careering past the Porta San Pancrazio,
        some with flags flying, in a riot of color
                and twinkling chrome and blaring horns,
                and I stood and cheered each one's

jaunty, rounded beauty, its buzzing revs
    and sewing-machine engine, the driver folded
behind the wheel, as if somehow all that moves
        could move me, till, with a smell of badly combusted
                fuel, it cracked itself, a gaudy whip,
                and wound away, like the end of a cartoon strip,

through the ancient city, ignoring the place
    where one of that number, colored midnight-blue
and eaten by rust, has not moved in many years,
        but waits, a sort of monument or memento,
                on half-inflated tires chocked with stone,
                with a basalt paver or a plaque of travertine.

A hydra head of wires on the dashboard
    where the tiny speedometer should be,
the windshield wiper blades long ago pilfered,
        it stands under the canes of wild blackberry
                in an angle of the Papal Wall,
                not sheltered by it because not vulnerable.

How long ago, on what routine morning,
    did someone, maybe late for work, park here

and hurry off, with the intent of returning,
  of course, remembering to lock the door,
      having tossed in, almost an afterthought,
      this dove-gray spiral notebook on the backseat

where now I look in as if at a monstrance,
  longing to open it at last and see—
what? Reckonings of pi, the heart's hundred veins,
  a list of emperors down to our own day,
      or on a page alone, now water-stained
      and written in an ordinary hand,

Color and motion all will come to this.
  The city knows it, has known it forever.
Through brick and tufa walls constantly pass
  bright threads of your life that can draw no closer
      the coasts of joy, through August's brutal sun
      and through the volleys of the autumn rain.

Janiculum Passage

This morning the sun rose behind a crown of spires
at St. John Lateran, the city in its bowl
still delicate with mist as the autumn deepened
after rain all night, and I saw a girl, her knees
closed against the flanks of her *motorino*,
her long hair flowing away beneath her helmet,
who, as she coasted the summit of that long hill,
the two-stroke raucous beneath her, bearing her on,
turned her head for just a moment, acknowledging
the view all the way from Monte Mario to
where the sun had avoided stranding itself in
the sky-blue cat's cradle of gasworks to the south.

Tiber Island

I went down to the Tiber Island
when autumn was quite far advanced,
the days short and the sycamore leaves brittle,
because someone I knew was ill,
and the place was sacred to healing.

Beside the polluted river,
I found the god's head and robed shoulders
and his winged staff wound with serpents
still carved into a travertine wall,
but time had sheared his face away.

A murmuration of starlings
was diffused in the clear air of evening
like black smoke or a blot of ink,
while a man in a respirator and a white jumpsuit
broadcast hawk noises through a megaphone,

lest the ten thousand shifting shapes
cohere in the limbs of a sycamore,
soiling everything beneath them,
disfiguring the palm and the stone pine.
Again and again the harsh cry

launched itself against a percolating mass
that seemed to yield, teeming with voices
and the ungodly rustle of wings,
but then simply stood on its side,
like a grand piano up a spiral staircase,

and coiled off to re-form somewhere else,
through the apricot-streaked evening air,
jeering, dented, healing quickly,
with a torque that arose from earth itself,
in hourglass shapes and nightmare trapezoids

and ugly memes. It was hopeless to oppose them,
though the death-pale man continued,
even when he could no longer see
what it was that he hoped to disperse,
which had become identical with the dark.

Janiculum Staircase

In a daylight facade of closed shutters,
    one window is always open,
    giving onto a modest kitchen,
        tidy, with a bowl of fruit
    that seems to change according to the season,
that ripens and matures.
        The bananas are my favorite.

I have never seen a person in that room,
    though the dishrag is folded and neat
    on the long neck of the sink faucet.
        But someone must live there, someone cares
    that a passing stranger should have a glimpse of it,
a tranquility that seems far removed from
        the city and its dirt and noise.

I am given this glimpse every day,
    and never without a sense of trespass,
    though the fruit could be made of stone, of course,
        in this kitchen that floats in midair,
    visible only from a staircase
descending in zigzags to Trastevere,
        since the apartment is on the third floor.

That staircase smells of human things,
    of things nocturnal and intimate
    flyblown by day and indifferent:
        the leavings of compulsion, pleasure, both.
    And from the rich soil of that excrement,
from its corruption and its nourishings,
        figs and tomato seedlings have sprung forth;

so perhaps that kitchen is a mere antechamber
    to some other place intent with life, some
    fully inhabited inner room,
        could I look past the fruit made of stone
    and my own constant longing to succumb
to the emptiness of modesty and order,
        while descending the stairs into town.

III

North Frieze Block XLVIII, Figures 118–20

We know they lived short lives in a world of slavery:
is this why their faces are so beautiful and grave,
one wearing a soft cap, pooled at his shoulders,
another naked, the line of his back
like a tornado's funnel, in a monochrome canter
riding into the gruel and blizzard of time
that has scoured even their tack away,
three young men, their mounts superb beneath them,
cheek pressed to throatlatch in a curve so powerful
it will never come unsprung, even in the explosion
of their own stalled momentum, veins on their bellies
and hocks and forearms standing in pure joy,
reined in at the last possible moment
before plunging off the edge and into eternity?

The Stones at the Circus Maximus

It's nice to be playing in a place that's older than we are.

—MICK JAGGER

Scorpus won two thousand chariot races
before he died at the age of twenty-seven,
but these ones have not gotten the word
that all things crumble and fade.
The choicest stone was robbed out,
the whole place buried in river silt
and the obelisks hauled somewhere else
after the last games in 549.

No one dares throw down curse amulets
against these ancient riders.
The crowd loves them, wants to move like them,
wants to thread the labyrinth out of time.
Straddling her boyfriend's shoulders, a girl
makes a hybrid beast charging the stage, while
with bandannas, earrings, and bracelets,
they pout and stalk through bread and circuses,

dressed in charioteers' livery:
red for war and green for April,
blue for sea and sky, and white
for the wind. One moves like midnight,
with the stealth of the panther that died
here snarling to amuse a crowd
long since gone to dust now borne feelingly
in little devils around the smashed marble

where two bodies were entwined
on the scuffed earth yesterday.
One was wearing flame-colored running shoes
and had the head of a faun, of Caravaggio's
ruined boys or Pasolini's lover.
They pressed the bent purple flower
and the parched grass, forlorn and defiant,
perpendicular to the racetrack's long straightaway,

while near the triumphal gate
commemorating Titus's conquest of Jerusalem,
a vendor had positioned his awning
against the sun of a summer morning,
and in each small concentric metal dish
for a trickle of water to refresh
was a fragment of coconut—
never quite as good when you taste them.

A Pair of Fountains

1. Ask a Question

This is the one
who does not even know how to ask a question.
Morning light
flushes the bellows of his cheeks as it
glazes each bead
of water from his pursed lips in the thread
falling into
a half basin of travertine below,
necessity
wrinkling his brow with what he cannot say:
the rhetoric
of other fountains, all their euphuistic
surge and flow
escape him, humble last child, and with no
proud tricolor
intended where rust-red and slime-green gather,
although, in autumn,
when plane leaves clog the grate and make it brim
and briefly flood,
some passersby may see the fountain, nod
to the hydrocephalous
goodwill abundant in this man-child's face,
his eyes asquint,
and bend, and drink, and realize what is meant
by thirst is all
other than what fame teaches; at this wall
know, and for sure,
the sweetest water is the most obscure.

2. Starry Crown

—for Rosanna Warren

A girl yawns like a cat beside the fountain,
an old Pope's muscle in the gouts and spatter,
love-muscle in the plashing and the glitter.

Girl and fountain do not love each other.
Both are beautiful and both are vain.
She loves the water for its reflection.

A black cat stretches indolent in the sun
that gloves it lithely as if in silver
against the scarred volutes of travertine

on an old church. The young priest at the corner
stands in a quandary in his soutane,
caught in the glowing throat of afternoon,

clasped to her breast by Rome the giant mother
as is the pleb near the Gemonian Stair,
at his feet lute-shaped seeds of the sail pine,

beads of sweat like jewels in his black hair,
and the young man dressed in a wedding gown
and sneakers who, past flowering oleander,

unsteadily waltzes a mannequin,
busty and nude, down a runway of beer
while his friends shout *O carità Romana!*

Each private soul, carried to full and over-
full, falls at last to its disintegration
beyond the rolled edge of a starry crown

with little subsiding noises of passion,
applause that fades in a descending patter,
as evening comes and once more sacks the town.

Stumbling Blocks: For Pius XII

(after Gunter Demnig's commemorative project *Stolpersteine*)

At the end of *Roma città aperta* by Rossellini,
    after the SS officer has given the coup de grâce
to the Catholic priest played by Aldo Fabrizi,

the scab-kneed children who have watched through the fence
    troop downhill and St. Peter's is in the background,
its dome floating like a miracle they do not notice.

Sampietrini, Rome's cobblestones are called,
    and like a tooth or a nail hand forged at a smithy,
they taper, top to bottom. Bedded in sand,

their flat crowns are laid in fans whose radii,
    it is said, are those of a workman's outstretched arm,
the reach of what a man can do in a day.

They make the tires of passing cars buzz and hum,
    and shake the city buses almost to pieces,
that must slow to a crawl, passing over them.

They retain heat during the long summers,
    and are slippery underfoot with autumn rain.
In the book of Matthew, chapter 16, Christ says,

"Upon this rock I will build" to Simon Bar-Jonah,
    "and the gates of hell shall not prevail against it."
Outside certain buildings, the cobbles have been

struck into gold, like a myth or a judgment.
     Inscribed on each, spelled out letter by letter,
is HERE LIVED . . . with a birth date and a death date.

Arrested on New Year's Day 1944,
     and deported to Mauthausen, Giacomo Spizzichino
was murdered on April 19 of the next year.

Arrested five months later, his brother Eugenio
     was deported to Auschwitz, and after January 20
murdered in an unknown place (*in luogo ignoto*).

Their home was here, at 47 Via Goffredo Mameli.
     And Augusto Sperati was arrested just before Christmas
as a political prisoner, in 1943,

and murdered at Hartheim Castle, near Linz.
     Someone dug up his cobble last week
and replaced it—as if no one would notice—

with an ordinary gray basalt rock,
     as if history were simply a matter
of what is removed, revised, held back:

but you cannot step on their graves, which are in the air,
     and the beam in your eye, you cannot lift it so.
Without walking, how will you get from here to there?

And the more you walk on them, the brighter they glow.

IV

Troia

—for David Rubin

Ruined Troy lay promiscuous among
    findspot and tell, breastworks and ditches
like nine gold bracelets at a Turkish wedding,
        in twenty-two carats, mined outside Pergamum.
Schliemann's trench was a wound through the whole thing:
    at the Scaean Gate he was off by twelve hundred years,

where the mourning doves sang compulsively,
    vulgar-throated. In the music's pause
near two stone griffins, a feral tabby
        warmed herself on a broken plinth, almond blossom
made a blizzard in the orchard nearby,
    and the spokes of wild fennel crossed with the sun's rays.

The Scamander River was nowhere to be seen,
    having wandered off across
the rich alluvial plain. Nothing more would happen,
        that was the spirit and the sum:
nothing would happen here ever again;
    that, a taste of fennel, and the goat bells' tinnitus.

Stromboli

(*Odyssey* X, 1–87)

He married his six daughters to his six sons,
according to the economy of the place,
for those who were there were destined not to leave.
The cliffs of obsidian rose sheer from sea to sky.
He received us with generosity, listened to what we said,

the low pipes moaning through the court all day,
the thorn-tongued cactus hemmed with crystal after rain,
pink oleander flowers crushed on the cement.
The place rewarded us and yet remained apart
in its austere contempt for all who voyaged.

I walked beyond the elephant-legged geranium,
bleached by the sun and taller than a man,
the four o'clocks, their long throats yearning open,
beyond the thistle, lentisk, and mountain laurel;
and in a canton of sterile soil made rich

with salts from the deep nether earth,
where fumaroles kept their white sentinels
below a citadel of crystal sulfur,
I saw the branching wranglers' horns of goats
as they devoured the flower of the broom

in long coats smelling of goat, and in their eyes
I saw no place for myself on that island.
All night a shawl of red-hot lapilli
erupted into the air at intervals
in crimson threads like those of the caper flower,

cascading down, cartwheeling into a sea
that on the third day held torn linen in its mouth,
the wind from the northwest, the shallows muttonfat jade.
Our ship hoisted herself up on her blue elbows
and roared away with a plume and a splatter of salt.

All that had been given was proof against return:
that was the rule, I knew it. The very narrative
he coaxed out of us, those evenings, led to him
only because it also led away.
His was not an island we were meant to see again.

Aeaea

At that hour when the onshore breeze
 drove the waves of panting crystal
onward over the ribbed sand,
 tugging their shadows beneath them
toward the pastel hotel,
 and the light-shot shallows were marbled
with the first premonitions of autumn,
 I said to the beach chair attendant,
to the one colored Etruscan-red
 with a boar's head tattooed on his shoulder,
I said, as the ball of the sun
 lowered itself moment by moment
with an almost erotic delay
 toward the steep sides of an island
standing off on the horizon,
 I said—Could you please tell me
the name of that island? And he smiled
 and said to me—That is no island,
but the headland of Monte Circeo,
 for the bay curves far past Terracina
to where, in one of forty-three caves,
 the witch Circe lived with Odysseus
after he had eaten the lily leek,
 the golden garlic, the Syrian rue,
and out of the vowels of its name,
 she bore him a son, Telegonus,
who founded the city Praeneste,
 where the Temple of Fortuna Primigenia
still lies open against the hillside
 like the body of her the hero loved.

But the island, man—the island is in your mind.
                         By this time the sun was disappearing
into a kind of black crater,
                         and it made me want to cry out,
as the shadows climbed out of the sea
                         and color drained from the sides of the hotel,
so I turned to him, but the chairs were folded,
                         the sand cold, night coming on.

Argos

Every morning in the park of broken statues,
a group of dog walkers gathers,

among them a woman with short steel-gray hair
in a purple fleece, a chain-smoker,

the head of the CGL, someone told me,
one of the most powerful union bosses in Italy.

We have never spoken to each other—
I am no one to her, just another tall foreigner

in a gray tracksuit, and she is always moving her hands,
absorbed in conversation with her friends

while the dogs mill around (the class clown,
the diva, the troublemaker, the lonely sensitive one)—

but when she calls to her dog, an Alsatian, magnificent,
black and gold, all the others are silent,

and even the nymph fleeing a satyr pauses,
and the sphinx, rolling a skull beneath her paws,

to contemplate loyalty amid complicated politics.
Argos! Argos! The hero's dog, infested with ticks

and cast away to die on the dunghill,
but the noble lines in him still unmistakable,

and Odysseus, twenty years gone, brushes a tear away,
careful that no one else should see.

Circe

There are pigs up the road a mile.
         I visit them every day.
         Under a turning maple tree,
they lie in the sun in a pile,

then rouse themselves to a quorum,
         jostling and biting each other
         (they don't smell too good either),
as if to say: "Thank God you've come!

Just tell us what to do."
         And I ask them at the fence:
         "Was any of you a man once?"
because one has eyes that are blue,

like the eyes of another in whom I found—
         half my life I had known him—not a hint
         of recognition, some ravishment
having erased me from his mind;

or one I had known, walking past me,
         who shook the memory off
         in the street as if chiding himself,
and bit his lip gently.

Yesterday I went around back
         on the sloping concrete apron
         poured beside the barn
not long ago by the ready-mix truck:

and instead of the dirty dutiful gaze,
        there atop a mess of offal,
          red liver and coiled blue-green bowel,
were two hacked heads in a heaped grimace

of bristle and yellow teeth and squinting,
        shameless, heavy and sweet in that yard,
        and my question was answered.
The pigs knew who did it but weren't telling.

A Letter from Istanbul

1
March 19, 20—

My Dearest Son,
    I write to you from what Keats called "the realms of gold"
—not that he ever saw them, beyond the coffered ceiling

and its gilded rosettes, from his deathbed on Piazza di Spagna
in a mean small room now echoing with the shouts of drunken students.

Nor do I mean Greece, where your grandfather, a straitlaced man,
experienced, I believe, a kind of sensual epiphany

in August of the year 1972.
Under the dictatorship, he had taken us

to the island of Lemnos in the northern Aegean,
where the forge god Hephaestus once fell to earth,

cast out of Olympus, and where the archer Philoctetes
howled with pain from his suppurating foot.

    My father belonged to the generation of World War II,
for whom talking about feelings was a kind of anathema,

but in February of that year, my mother had died,
leaving him broken; and something in the beauty of that place,

in the contrast between the parched earth and the sea's aquamarine,
led him to say to me, —I hope you have the chance

to be here once in your life with someone you love;
and I don't mean just the physical part, either.

I was startled by his candor, being of an age,
you understand, when the slightest thing could arouse me:

the smell of figs, or of wastewater on the garden,
or the cool stone floor beneath an empty bed.

   By that time, my father was speaking out of the memory
of what he had had and lost, rather than the thing itself—

love, I mean: for I believe he and my mother
did love each other, though they made each other unhappy;

but in any case, it was as if two parts of his own nature
had been explained to him for the first time,

body and spirit, by some god of that barren place,
so that in his voice were both a kind of wonder

and an unaccustomed severity,
since he knew I was already eager to experience love,

although I did not know the costs; and he knew
that all his love could not spare me from those costs.

   2

   Instead, I thought of you in the Church of Saint Savior in Chora
here in the Golden Horn, on a spring morning

—or rather, I thought of your having told me,
on the Palatine in Rome, one hot July afternoon,

that you hated being with art in the presence of crowds,
that you hated being a tourist; and at the time, I responded

that I have spent my life following beauty,
but have seldom managed to be its sole audience.

    In this fresco, for instance, Christ hales Adam and Eve
out of their graves with an unholy physical roughness,

in an *Anastasis*, a Harrowing of Hell,
and though there were tourists who looked on imperturbably,

repeating the image over and over in their photographs,
diffusing it into a cloud of data, an atmosphere,

a sensorium on which other consumers could feed,
I would not have denied it to myself for the presence of others.

    I saw locks in the Topkapi Palace, their wards oiled and intricate,
that in this fresco seem to lie shattered under Christ's feet,

as if a camera had been dropped on the floor,
all its stored images suddenly inaccessible,

its parts foolish, in their ingenious articulation,
before the original and its primary awe,

the gates of Hell broken down for once and for all,
and Satan bound up tight, like the hapless fly

in a spider's web. Belief might come like that,
explosive and rapt, once or twice in a lifetime,

but in my experience it is more often the product
of long study and a loving routine,

as in the mosaic of the Virgin caressed as a child
by her parents, who were older parents, and who perhaps thought

as we did, before we were given that sacred trust,
that they were not going to be parents at all,

Anna and Joachim, but then were given it.
We have tried to give you love with the force of *almost-was-not*.

3

I wonder whether it is true that we come full circle,
in our lives, and end more or less where we began.

In this mosaic of the Dormition of the Virgin,
Christ cradles the soul of Mary who is his mother,

container of the uncontainable,
and she is depicted as an infant in swaddling clothes,

while under the feet of saints spring crimson poppies,
and in the pendentives there are gorgeous peacocks,

the bird that is the symbol of incorruptibility,
as we once saw them at the Cathedral of Saint John the Divine

in New York City, not far from where your maternal grandmother
now lies diapered in her final illness,

her confusion varying according to the opiates
she is given against the chronic pain.

On the path leading to the Topkapi Palace,
there was a cypress tree, the tree of mourning,

split by the trunk and branches of a fig,
the fig growing from the midriff of the cypress,

the fruit of the body from the dark wood of grief,
as in the *Dream of the Virgin* by Simone dei Crocefissi,

where the Tree of Life on which Christ is crucified
grows from the womb of the Virgin on her deathbed

while a companion sitting beside her reads to her,
for perhaps she is not dying, perhaps she is just asleep.

    And here Christ heals the woman with an issue of blood.
My mother was often sick with female troubles

during my childhood, but there was also depression,
some days so bad that she could not get out of bed.

I once saw a painting of Saint Margaret of Antioch
who, having been swallowed by a demon, hacked her way out

with the help of a simple wooden cross.
I heard someone say my mother's demons got her in the end,

but she had good days and bad days, like anyone else.
What she needed was Saint Margaret's wooden cross.

4

    I do not know the medium in which you will read this,
except it must be adequate to the primacy of my love.

I want this letter to be a shorthand between us,
like the quotations from old screen comedies

we bandy back and forth to raise a smile:
a set of cues, a way of recovering the years

that have intervened by now to separate us
irrevocably from your infancy and childhood;

a closed system, then, a human artifact
proof against the insinuations of eternity:

for if even two of us, caught as we are in time,
understand that spirit may be reached through the body

by which we apprehend the beauty of this world,
then there is hope for everyone else as well.

When Sinan built the Süleymaniye Mosque, he created
capture-places in the dome for the smoke that rose upward

from candles illuminating the prayers of the faithful.
This smoke, being mixed with egg, was made into ink

for those writing scripture in the nearby *medrese*:
so the light and breath of those prayers became their text.

And workmen repairing the keystone of an aqueduct
in a suburb north of Istanbul once found a bottle

containing Ottoman script. It was a message from Sinan,
who had long been dust, saying the keystone

would need to be replaced after four hundred years,
and it specified the type and source of the stone.

But most of us lack such foresight, lack a system:
we cannot face down time like an architect.

It is fear I see, in the eyes of Adam and Eve,
confronted with Christ in his robes of dazzling white,

who grabs each by the wrist: fear, and the reluctance
of those who are dead and then called back to life.

They had sinned and had grown accustomed to sinning,
just as we habituate ourselves, over the years,

until we cannot imagine another course.
It is art that hales us out of our graves,

if the Christian mystery is unavailable—
for I know that we have given you no belief

except the *capacity* to believe, over a lifetime;
and though I once knew a poet of a very great age

who boasted that he had never written a poem
about a work of art, this seems perverse.

     Beauty is an avenue to belief,
realized in art and what we can take from it.

By art, I do not mean Demetrios's silver idols
of Diana at Ephesus, against which the Apostle Paul

railed in the theater until they shouted him down,
for those were mere duplicates of a lost original,

nothing inhering in them of that first great power,
like the photographs made by those solemn tourists,

exhalations into an atmosphere of image.
I mean something altogether more ineffable,

uniting body and spirit for a moment.
Perhaps it was this your grandfather was referring to

long ago, when he spoke to me with wonder
and yearning, he in whom so much seemed unexamined;

for landscape can do it too, as well as art:
provide a medium for our only true life.

Would you be an artist? Oh, my beloved son,
you must witness beauty then; you must let it speak

and tell it over to yourself and others—
cross, cloud, keystone, peacock, poppy, shattered wards,

blood's issue, cypress, fig—wherever you find it,
though few will understand what you are doing.

I thought of you in this ancient church: that is all.
I send you my love and hope to see you in the summer.

VI

Santa Cecilia

It is Saturday morning, and my errand is to buy marmalade
    from the grumpy nuns at Santa Cecilia in Trastevere
    (Cecilia, who told Valerian on their wedding day
that an angel was watching over her maidenhead).

I think of slipping into San Francesco a Ripa,
    where they've made a broom closet out of De Chirico's tomb chapel,
    and Bernini's *Blessèd Ludovica Albertoni* is all
in her ecstasy, but I see men outside shouldering up a

glossy wooden box, and I hear bell metal struck,
    tolling a note and then the minor third below,
    the music of the end, even on a morning aglow
like this one, with the Tiber running high, colored coffee-and-milk,

pressing against the walls of the embankment: so I continue
    without delay to Santa Cecilia, where lapis lazuli
    and gilded pomegranates attend the sculpted effigy
of a girl sleeping her perpetual sleep under the baldachino,

and only the gently weeping line on her neck
    and something uncanny about the rotation
    of her head, under its covering napkin,
suggest that she will not, after all, awake

to another ordinary day in paradise,
    the apse mosaics studded with dates from a palm,
    while, on an upper branch, a phoenix bursts into flame,
lambs leave the Holy City single file, and an ancient nun is

picking out a melody on the organ keyboard
  while still wearing, I notice, her bedroom slippers.
  But my errand is marmalade from the fruit of the trees
in the cloister garden, so she must be interrupted:

One jar, please, yes, with light enough in it
  to last the winter, and not sweet but bitter,
  with homunculus shapes adrift in its cloudy ichor,
cut from the astringent and salvific fruit.

Chiaraviglio

Three green birds sit
in a green tree
in the month of January.

Each has chewed the crown
out of an orange
and leisurely

extracts the juice and seeds:
three bright green birds
sipping orange juice

above the fallen column,
the pitted cherub's face
and carved acanthus altar

splashed with their lime.
They bob and sway
atop each jagged hull,

each broken, sucked-out wheel
and mildewed felly,
boisterous viridian

quaffing the bittersweet,
and though a hooded crow,
sable-winged, slate-vested,

nearby yells *Cras, cras, cras,*
these do not care,
for like the phoenix bird

that rides the palm of Paradise
in a mosaicked vault,
long-tailed they have drunk

the juice of paradise,
and will not taint themselves
with lesser darknesses.

Defiant eye, black beak,
how gorgeously they rise
and in discordant thirds

quarter the unwarm sky,
leaving these broken lamps
aloft upon the dusk.

A Roman Garden

Last night I dreamed again I was his son
    (searching always for fathers, orphan of sleep),
then woke to hear hooded crows in the rain
    whose raucous cries reverberated deep
within the garden and its citrus grove
    laden with chill and pebble-rinded fruit.
He who is not my father does not move,
    but waits; far from here, he could speak, but does not.
Some lamps to light the dark of where he is:
    my hand reached out. But then the eyeless bald
ivory skull and gleaming nightmare feathers
    mocked me. I could bring nothing to the world.
The crows flew off beyond my furthest thought,
as citrus cast its heavy perfumed light.

VII

Santa Maria in Trastevere

—for Emily Wallace

The master got it right and wrong, as usual.
  In the gloom, he wrote, *the gold gathers*
  the light against it, which is true, as far as
inroads of darkness go, the perpetual

rebuff of night required of these mosaics;
  and yet, even as I raise my binoculars
  toward the apse, the art is greater than this,
as centuries of homicidal ethics,

when realized as a diurnal fact,
  make a mere granular paste and deliquesce
  before the legend and its tenderness
that brims and overwhelms the sight—an instinct,

really, a fierce unquenchable nuclear core,
  as Christ says to her, COME, MY CHOSEN ONE
  AND I SHALL PLACE THEE UPON MY THRONE.
Flank to flank, mother and son are lovers:

nothing can match this in eternity.
  HIS LEFT HAND SHOULD BE UNDERNEATH MY HEAD,
  the Virgin replies, AND HIS RIGHT HAND SHOULD
EMBRACE ME, no sentiment, no vulnerability,

claiming what is her right without reproof,
  co-regnant with him in a vault of gold,
  in stiff jeweled robes. The master should have told
something of *this* mortal-immortal love.

Two Farewells

1. A *Narcissus*

(in memory of Seamus Heaney, 1939–2013)

I led you that day through the gallery,
or so I thought, a smiling public man,
now slowed a little, but good-naturedly
revisiting the classics one by one—
Raphael's mistress; wronged Beatrice Cenci—
as if in a kind of valediction,
testing them on your life, finding them true
or not: but in fact I was led by you.

And only gradually did I realize
that there was more. You were looking for something,
beyond the gilded swag of centuries,
the amazements of Da Cortona's ceiling
or of Borromini's spiral staircase,
and your wise passiveness was all pretending.
But *what?* What was it made you go canny,
each image charged, set to go off, maybe?

Not the calm of *Saint Francis in Meditation,*
nor the deep tribal hatred of *Judith
Beheading Holofernes,* the old crone
beside the aroused girl so intent with
revenge, set to receive, in jubilation,
the gory trophy in her rough brown cloth,
the white bed linen webbed in ropes of blood.
Such violence you had known and rejected.

The enchantress Circe wasn't it, either,
who transformed men to pigs (but you remained
unchanged) and Picus into a woodpecker
for jealousy of his wife, who at the end,
in grief at losing him, became all water
and vanished on the breeze; whose song returned
birds to their branch and moved rocks: after all,
there was no time for such a pretty fable.

At last you stopped before a darker place,
being the world's mirror, the self's deep lake,
where a lovely boy swooned at his own pale face,
his knee bent so that it looked anamorphic,
his doublet richly figured, and it was,
in that moment, as if you had to check—
the only time I saw your face grow stern—
one last thing, then nod slightly and move on.

2. Villa Aurora

(in memory of John Hollander, 1929–2013)

To the garden of the Texas beauty queen's
Roman villa (ex-*Playboy* centerfold
and Daughter of the American Revolution)
we were summoned one afternoon to plant a cherry
on Washington's Birthday, noble and common
assembled to a sound of distant thunder;

or perhaps it was instead the sly thunder
of hooves from a statue (half-concealed by flowering quince)
of Priapic Pan, its common
attribution to Michelangelo, the sweet fold
between some nymph's legs, the attainable cherry,
having aroused it to a bawdy revolution,

wicked through the years' long revolution,
leering, indifferent to the little thunder
as we each put a shovelful of earth on the roots of the cherry,
hoping rain would hold off, and the Paphian Queen's
body shone nearby in one of her manifold
poses, our radiant hostess, in a silent come-on,

while we stood nonplussed on her private common
and she invoked the Daughters of the American Revolution
as liveried footmen belatedly did unfold
chairs for dignitaries, and the distant thunder
registered as concern on the beauty queen's
flawless face as she addressed the spindling cherry

("O Tree!") for all of us who had grown chary
of rain and speeches and the common
tree-planting—though even commoner, in Queens,

New York, where I stand now, is the revolution
that with modest ceremony and without thunder
puts a poet in the ground, in the earth's fold.

No more walks in the wood, no more poems to unfold,
no more sharp ax to the trembling cliché of cherry,
no more righteous thunder
against the self-important ones who would make common
fraud instead pass for true revolution,
just a raw wooden box and a hole in the ground in Queens

with a dead thunder of earth on it, the common
cherry weeping nearby at this revolution
so far from our bedraggled fold at the beauty queen's.

VIII

Gentle Joyous God

In this season, I think of Dionysus and the pirates
    as they might be on a black figure vase,
the ship's mast wreathed with grapevines, and the flutes
    shrilling out their Lydian madness

as men tumble overboard, their bodies mingled with
    those of muscled dolphins violet with spray,
heavy as the hanging panicles of wisteria
    or a body part dandled toward your mouth,

while threaded through it all is the perfume
    of flesh in peonies, gathering until
at last you must bury your face in them,
    then fall back blowsy in a nest of petal

as the sleepy boy, the gentle joyous one,
rouses himself in the garden after days of rain.

Reading Apuleius

—for Corey Brennan

In 1933, midsummer,
    vexed by the ablative absolute,
she looks toward the camera,
    behind her the dark oak wainscot

of the library reading room,
    two spinsters on her left-hand side.
She has learned each colleague's name
    as protocol and place demanded,

Faulsporn, Ogle, Solliman,
    Van Kulp, Keck, Queef: the fellowship,
gifted and dull. To her concern,
    her recent thought has seemed to slip.

Her husband is the Annual Professor,
    bespectacled, already bald,
in a light suit, standing behind her.
    With one hand, she could touch and hold—

And certain Latin lines run riot
    (that girl with a firebrand between her thighs),
whenever she would concentrate
    (or the one who couples with an ass),

while figs are oozing in the garden:
    their burst sockets and rosy flesh,
mosquitoes at her ankles, noon . . .
    She muses, chin in hand. The wish

leads like the buttons on her sweater
in a wayward diagonal
beyond the frame of this picture.
Her smile is mocking, dreamy, carnal.

Pentecost

For five days you had a cold in your eye,
the gray of your gaze gone bloody.
The fire brigade climbed the bald dome
and through the circle of the oculus
dumped a cascade of rose petals.

Joseph surnamed Justus did not call,
so we were eleven after all,
and the cloven-footed flame
was nearly transparent in daylight
as we prepared the noon meal.

A rosemary bush flourished upward,
splitting the carved acanthus pediment,
as a little dog ran atop the wall,
one leg lame, barking hysterically,
beside the gate which is called Beautiful

and the perpetual fountain.
We were all drunk on new wine,
the spirit poured out, something labile,
while wind rushed through strakes of the umbrella pine.
Everyone heard in his own tongue,

Parthian and Mede and Elamite,
and we called each other by name
as our children played not far off.
We were pricked to the heart
and had all things in common,

at least it felt that way for a while.

IX

Fiumicino, Morning

Effortlessly the buzzard strokes
    the midway air,
    each wingtip's splayed feather
    darkly visible where,
above the concrete apron

and the parched earth
    splashed with poppies
    and those flowers known as
    the eyebrows of Zeus,
it tilts and rides the thermals,

above the runway's game board
    shapes of the geometer,
    cone and cylinder,
    dihedral, rhombus, delta,
whose skin-deep miracles of surface

sufficed for us to fly,
    as a blue-suited man
    puts his head in the mouth of an engine
    that has crossed an ocean,
turns away, and pops a Pez in his mouth.

Ostia Antica

Down the *decumanus maximus*
    till the rutted cobbles give way,
just as so many lives have gone before this,
    past the stubs of the *insulae*,

while each Airbus at Fiumicino
    heaves itself aloft
over the beach umbrellas in row on row
    where the Tyrrhenian Sea laps, soft;

and I, too, have felt Rome drop astern
    of that imperative bound west,
have settled back and been home by afternoon.
    But this time I smell the dust

and heat as I walk an open field
    to Room 16, Trench 3, Layer 3,
where he works, my tousle-headed man-child,
    sifting broken plaster and tesserae

to recover a hippocamp in the sun,
    a taurocamp, a pardalocamp in monochrome,
or six bulked-up charioteers from the age of Constantine,
    each with a trophy cylinder and a name:

for they, too, had dreams of motion and flight,
    their cool vaults of pine-green and ocher
just fragments, rubbed to color with a little spit
    in the province of the dumpy level and weak mortar,

where the Tiber still wanders toward the sea,
    now several kilometers distant;
and when I am judged, as I will be,
    whatever I achieved or intended,

at the end of my own days,
    may it be by one as tender and meticulous
with his sharp trowel and soft brushes,
    in his faded sweat-stained clothes.

A Return

The tenants will not renew:
    the house will stand empty.
    All the childhood fears come over me,
the moves every year or two,

the family broken as a family,
    the heartsick burden of place
    dragged through continents and cities,
the constant anonymity,

the weird dislocated shame.
    Then, standing before a door painted
    the color of dried blood,
my father appeared in a dream,

who gave me the little he could
    (and for all that, it was enough)
    out of his own fear and love,
he with whom life did what it wanted,

now twenty-five years gone,
    with his limping gait and his game smile,
    both resolute and vulnerable,
wearing a sweater colored fawn

like any hunted thing.
    Impulsively I embraced him:
    his body was solid and warm,
but the air was alive with his perishing,

or rather, it was as if he had put
    the seals on one house, on all houses,
    in which, through a velvet darkness,
motes glittered in a column of sunlight.

Father, when shall I join you in that kingdom,
    as you stand in front of a door
    closed on so much empty air?
And how shall I know it is home?

Roma città aperta

At the end of *Roma città aperta* by Rossellini,
    after the SS officer has given the coup de grâce
to the Catholic priest played by Aldo Fabrizi,

the scab-kneed children who have watched through the fence
    troop downhill, and St. Peter's is in the background,
its dome floating like a miracle they do not notice.

I watched the movie again last night. Beyond
    my window were patches of filthy snow
as grudging winter yielded and spring returned;

but only when the bloody-handed thugs in the Via Tasso
    had tortured the Resistance leader to death
with the blowtorch, the pliers, the lash, and the priest was forced to

listen to his cries as others amused themselves with
    cognac and Chopin in another room
and the woman who betrayed him had fainted at the truth

in the fur coat they bought her for: as I say, it came
    only slowly, after the pregnant Anna Magnani
had been shot dead in the street in wartime Rome,

with a blot of crimson and a concussion of dismay
    like the red-bellied woodpecker in the catalpa hammering
at the reluctance of each lengthening day,

that dawn had broken, and it was Easter morning.

Airbus
Philosopher and mystic Giordano Bruno was burned at the stake for heresy by the Inquisition in 1600. The great Ticinese architect Francesco Borromini was Bernini's rival and died a suicide in 1667.

Body and Mask
Benvenuto Cellini (1500–1571) was a Florentine goldsmith, sculptor, and painter.

On the Janiculum, January 7, 2012
The poem begins with the first line of Wordsworth's sonnet "Composed Upon Westminster Bridge, September 3, 1802," describing London.

Tiber Island
Sacred to healing since antiquity, this island in the center of Rome now has a maternity hospital on it. The Greek god of healing, Aesculapius, is often depicted with a caduceus, a staff wound with serpents.

North Frieze Block XLVIII, Figures 118–20
This sonnet was written for an exhibition catalogue to accompany a watercolor of part of the Parthenon frieze by American artist Wendy Artin.

The Stones at the Circus Maximus
The concert described took place on June 22, 2014.

Starry Crown
The penultimate stanza of the poem paraphrases a line in Eleanor Clark's book *Rome and a Villa* (1952).

Stumbling Blocks: For Pius XII

Eugenio Pacelli was Pope Pius XII from 1939 to 1958. Although the Roman Catholic Church began the beatification process for him in 1964, his relationship with Nazi Germany and his attitude toward the Jews have been the subject of intense debate.

Troia

The archaeological site at Troy, in modern Turkey, consists of at least nine different excavated levels. Heinrich Schliemann (1822–1890) was a German entrepreneur and archaeologist. The Italian word *troia* also means "slut" or "trull."

Aeaea

After his visit and unwilling return to King Aeolus's island (imagined here as the Italian island of Stromboli), Odysseus stops at the island of Aeaea with his men on the way home from Troy. His men are turned into pigs by Circe, and then changed back at Odysseus's insistence.

A Letter from Istanbul

The poem's ideas about the reproduction of photographic images and the "sensorium" are indebted to designer Erik Adigard. The painting of Saint Margaret of Antioch is by Guercino (1644) and is in Arezzo. Mimar Sinan (1489–1588) was the great Ottoman architect. The episode with Paul and Demetrios is recounted in the Bible in Acts 19.

Santa Cecilia

Saint Cecilia, the patron of music and musicians, was martyred under Severus Alexander around 230 C.E. Stefano Maderno (1576–1636), like Borromini from Italian Switzerland, carved his beautiful statue of the uncorrupted body of Saint Cecilia as he saw it when her tomb was opened in 1599.

Chiaraviglio

Cras means "tomorrow" in Latin.

Santa Maria in Trastevere

The italicized phrase by Ezra Pound occurs at several places in the *Cantos*. The texts held by the figures in the mosaic are from the Song of Songs.

A *Narcissus*

The poem is set in the Palazzo Barberini in Rome; the *Narcissus* described at the end is by Caravaggio, as is the *Judith Beheading Holofernes*.

Reading Apuleius

The Latin prose writer Lucius Apuleius lived in North Africa in the second century C.E. His novel the *Metamorphoses* is also called *The Golden Ass*.

Pentecost

The poem includes language from Acts 2:1–31.

Ostia Antica

Ostia Antica was the ancient port city of Rome. It is across the Tiber River from Rome's airport at Fiumicino. The *decumanus maximus* was one of the main streets in a Roman town; *insulae* were blocks of apartment buildings. A "dumpy level" is a rudimentary surveying device. Hippocamp, taurocamp, and pardalocamp are, respectively, horse-, bull-, and leopardlike mythological creatures done in pavement mosaics.